EMERGENCY 999!
POLICE

Kathryn Walker
Photography by Chris Fairclough

WAYLAND

First published in 2011 by Wayland

Copyright © Wayland 2011

Wayland
338 Euston Road
London NW1 3BH

Wayland Australia
Level 17/207 Kent Street
Sydney, NSW 2000

Produced for Wayland by Discovery Books Ltd
Wayland series editor: Katie Powell
Editor: James Nixon
Designer: Ian Winton
Commissioned photography: Chris Fairclough

The author, publisher and Discovery Books Ltd would like to thank West Midlands Police for their help and participation in this book.

Picture credits: Shutterstock: pp. 4 (Solid Web Designs LTD), 6 top (Andrey Shadrin), 6 bottom (Martin Anderson), 7 top (Uwe Pillat), 26 bottom; Warwickshire Police: p. 5; West Midlands Police: pp. 7 bottom, 8, 9, 10, 13, 14, 15 top, 16, 17, 18, 19, 20, 21, 26 top, 27, 28, 29 top.

British Library Cataloguing in Publication Data
Walker, Kathryn, 1957-
   Police. -- (Emergency 999)
   1. Police--Juvenile literature. 2. Assistance in
   emergencies--Juvenile literature.
   I. Title II. Series
   363.2'3-dc22
   ISBN: 978 0 7502 6253 8

Printed in China

Wayland is a division of Hachette Children's Books,
an Hachette UK company. www.hachette.co.uk

Note to parents and teachers: Every effort has been made by the Publishers to ensure that the websites in this book are suitable for children, that they are of the highest educational value, and that they contain no inappropriate or offensive material. However, because of the nature of the Internet, it is impossible to guarantee that the contents of these sites will not be altered. We strongly advise that Internet access is supervised by a responsible adult.

CONTENTS

WHAT IS A 999 EMERGENCY?

Sometimes people find themselves or see others in dangerous situations. They need expert help – fast! This is a 999 emergency. It requires help from the fire service, an ambulance, the coastguard or the police. Some emergencies may need more than one of these services.

Police!

A serious car accident, a burglary taking place or someone being attacked, are just some of the emergencies where the police can help. To get their help quickly, we phone 999.

When a road accident like this happens, police, ambulance and fire services may be needed.

When a 999 call is made, lots of people work hard to send help as soon as possible. Lives can be saved and criminals caught if the police can get to the emergency fast. By knowing when to phone 999, you can help to make this happen.

Police emergencies

You should call 999 and ask for the police when:
- there is a risk that someone may be seriously injured
- a crime is happening or about to happen
- there has been a serious road accident
- a child is missing.

If you see someone breaking into a car, you should call 999 straight away.

999 Notes

To report a crime or accident that is not an emergency, call your local police force's non-emergency number. By calling 999 at the wrong time, you could delay help getting to someone who urgently needs it.

MAKING A 999 CALL

When you phone 999, an operator answers and asks 'Which service do you require?'. If you are not sure, tell the operator what has happened and he or she will decide for you.

Where are you?

When you call 999 from a **landline**, the number and address of your phone comes up on the operator's computer screen. Then if your call gets cut off, the operator knows where to send help. Calls from mobile phones are harder to trace. If you are using one, you need to say where you are calling from. If you are not sure, look for clues such as road names or landmarks.

Information on signposts can help you and the operator work out exactly where you are.

Some important points

All 999 calls are free and you can call from a mobile phone even if you have no credit. But remember, do not call 999 unless you really need to – making a **hoax** call is **illegal.**

When you call from an emergency roadside telephone, the operator will know your exact location.

999 Notes

In an emergency, 999 is not the only number you can phone. Calling 112 in the UK and most European countries will connect you to the emergency services. This is so that people travelling in Europe do not have to learn a different emergency number for each country they visit.

When the operator knows that you need the police, your call is put through to the police control centre.

POLICE CONTROL CENTRE

If you need the police, the operator puts your 999 call through to the police control centre for your area. The call taker there has to find out as much as possible about what is happening.

The call taker will ask:
- your name
- what has happened
- where the **incident** has happened or is happening
- if anyone is hurt.

Quick work

As the call taker is asking questions, he or she is keying the information into a computer system. This information is being passed to a **dispatcher**. The dispatcher's job is to contact police officers and send them to the emergency.

At the police control centre, call takers deal with thousands of calls each day.

Keeping you calm

A call taker may stay on the line until the police arrive. He or she may need to keep the caller calm or give important advice.

FACE-TO-FACE

Sade – Emergency Call Taker

I work 9-hour **shifts**, days and nights. A lot of calls turn out not to be real emergencies, but some do need urgent help. When a caller is in a very serious situation, I stay talking to help them through it. A long call can be exhausting and upsetting, so I can take a 'comfort break' – time to relax away from my desk.

To do this job, I need to make quick decisions about what to do. No two calls are the same, so the work is never boring.

ACTION!

The police control centre uses a computer system to keep track of where police officers are and what they are doing. A dispatcher radios the officers closest to an emergency, tells them where to go and gives them details of the incident.

The dispatcher stays in touch with the officers until the emergency is over. If extra help is needed, the dispatcher sends more officers.

Every second counts

Police cars have flashing lights and sirens to help them get to an emergency fast. When motorists see a flashing blue light or hear a siren wailing, they should pull over to let the vehicle through.

Police cars also have **satellite navigation (sat nav)** systems to help officers find their way to the incident.

radio

sat nav

keypad

When specific buttons on the keypad are pushed they activate the vehicle's sirens and flashing lights.

Inside a police car

Police cars always carry the following pieces of equipment that may be useful in an emergency:

- police tape – to seal off areas
- traffic cones and flashing lights
- emergency signs
- fire extinguisher
- first aid kit and blankets
- tools for breaking into buildings or cars
- broom and shovel, to clean up after a road accident.

999 Notes

When you make a 999 call, try to answer the questions as calmly and clearly as you can. Giving the call taker a good picture of what is happening and where you are will make sure that the right type of help is sent as fast as possible.

PREPARED AND PROTECTED

When uniformed officers leave the police station, they carry lots of important equipment. These items help them to do their job and protect them from injury. Police officers carry:

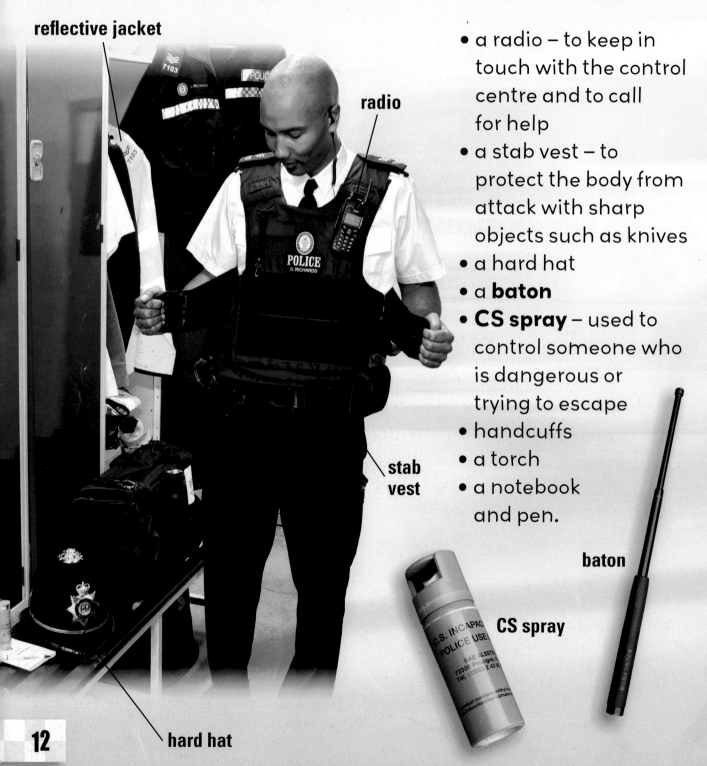

reflective jacket

radio

stab vest

hard hat

CS spray

baton

- a radio – to keep in touch with the control centre and to call for help
- a stab vest – to protect the body from attack with sharp objects such as knives
- a hard hat
- a **baton**
- **CS spray** – used to control someone who is dangerous or trying to escape
- handcuffs
- a torch
- a notebook and pen.

Armed police

In the United Kingdom, most police officers do not carry guns. However, some are specially trained to use guns and carry them when they go to a very dangerous incident. For example, armed police may be sent to **arrest** someone who has a dangerous weapon.

Police who guard or **patrol** places that need special protection, such as airports, also carry guns.

999 Notes

Some police officers now carry tasers. A taser is a weapon that gives a short electric shock. It does this either by shooting darts into the body or by being pressed against someone. A taser shock makes a person unable to move for a short time but does not kill or cause injury. Tasers are used by specially trained officers and only in dangerous situations.

Police cars are not the only vehicles that may be called to an emergency. Vans are used to carry extra officers, police dogs or when the police expect to arrest large numbers of people.

Police bikes

Police motorcycles may also be sent to emergencies, particularly road accidents. They can get through traffic faster than cars and are better for travelling down small lanes.

Help from above

If there is an emergency in an area far from a town, such as on farmland, police sometimes use helicopters. This is often the quickest way to send help. Police helicopters are also very useful for following cars or keeping track of criminals who are running from a crime scene.

The helicopters have **thermal imaging cameras** on board that can sense the heat from a person's body and find people in the dark. A police helicopter also has a powerful searchlight, strong enough to light up a whole football pitch.

A helicopter crew can search a large area much more quickly than police on the ground.

999 Notes

Each police car has a large number marked on its roof. This lets a helicopter in the sky identify police vehicles in an emergency.

WATER POLICE AND DIVERS

Not all emergencies and crimes take place on dry land. Areas where there is sea or a major waterway, such as a river or harbour, often have special police units called marine units or water police.

Policing the water

The water police are responsible for stopping crime on boats, banks and shores. They make sure that people using the waters stay safe and that the water traffic laws are obeyed. This is their main work, but they also take part in search and rescue operations on the water, often working with other emergency services.

Police boats are used to patrol canals too, like this one in a city centre.

Underwater officers

Marine units are made up of police officers trained to make searches of rivers, lakes and other waterways. They must dive underwater to search for the bodies of missing people, cars or stolen goods. Sometimes they search for **evidence**, such as weapons or clothes, that could help police solve a crime.

These specially trained police are wearing protective clothing to search a river. While one or two officers dive underwater the others stay on the surface.

999 Notes

The water police need to be well protected because waterways can contain many diseases. They wear dry suits to keep them clean and dry, gloves and full face masks when they dive. A **lifeline** attaches the diver to a person at the surface and the diver has radio contact with the rest of the team.

ANIMALS TO THE RESCUE

Emergency help sometimes comes on four legs –
when police dogs are called out. These highly trained
animals work with officers called police dog handlers.
Handlers learn how to use commands and signals to
let the dogs know what to do.

Follow that smell

Dogs have a much more powerful
sense of smell than humans. Police
dogs are trained to follow a person's
scent and find missing people
or criminals. Others sniff out
weapons, explosives or drugs.

This police dog is checking
for drugs in a block of flats.

Trained for trouble

It is not only a police dog's nose that makes it useful. Dogs can run faster than humans. On orders from its handler, a dog can chase someone running from a crime scene. It then uses its powerful jaws to hold the person until officers arrive.

FACE-TO-FACE

Dave – Police Dog Handler

My day starts early when I get up to feed and walk my dog, Max. Just before my shift begins, I load him into the van and get ready for patrol.

I get called to all sorts of incidents with Max. Sometimes we join officers who are chasing a criminal on foot. Other times we may help control someone who is violent. To do this job you must like dogs. Max and I work well together and trust each other completely.

FOLLOWING UP

When a crime or accident has taken place, Scenes of Crime Officers (SOCOs) may be called out. Their job is to collect evidence from the incident scene. This evidence may help the police discover who committed a crime and how.

Covered up

When SOCOs go to an incident scene, the area is taped off to keep people away (above). SOCOs sometimes wear paper suits that cover the whole body and rubber gloves (left). This stops dust, hair, fibres or anything else from their clothes and bodies getting mixed up with evidence at the scene.

A SOCO examines a crime scene area. Fibres, hairs or footprints could help solve a crime.

A SOCO (left) dusts with powder to show up fingerprints. The prints are lifted on tape so they can be examined in a laboratory (below).

Looking for clues

SOCOs take photos of injuries and incident scenes. They may also search for fingerprints. No two people have the same fingerprints, so any found at the scene may help the police prove that a particular person was there.

999 Notes

At a crime scene, SOCOs look for anything that has come from someone's body, such as hair, flakes of skin or drops of blood. Scientists then use **laboratory** equipment to look for **DNA** in this material. DNA is a substance found in the cells that make up a body. Apart from identical twins, no two people have the same DNA. So, if DNA found at a crime scene matches that of a **suspect**, it might prove that he or she committed the crime.

DETECTIVE WORK

Detectives are police officers, but they do not wear a uniform. They try to solve crimes and prove who committed them. To do this, detectives talk to **witnesses**, gather together facts and look for evidence.

This witness (left) tells the detective (right) about the crime he has seen.

At the station

Detectives work together in teams and share information. They are usually based in offices at police stations, where they work with uniformed police, SOCOs and other staff. Part of a detective's job is to question suspects at the police station.

Waiting and watching

Sometimes detectives have to spend long periods watching people in secret (left). They may do this to gather information or to get proof that someone is committing a crime. When a case goes to **court**, detectives must show the evidence that they have gathered.

FACE-TO-FACE

Craig – Detective

I spend part of my day investigating new cases. Then I'll talk to the victims and witnesses and take notes. If I have a suspect, I check through police files to see if we have information about that person.

When I think we have enough evidence to prove who committed a crime, I get it ready to take to court. It can be hard work getting to this point, but it's worth it when a criminal is found guilty.

AT THE STATION

The police station is the base or headquarters for police officers and other members of police staff. At the beginning of a shift, police officers gather in the parade room. This is where a **sergeant** tells them what has happened since they were last on duty and gives them their tasks.

A public place

The front desk at a police station is where the public visit or phone with questions and for advice. People go to the front desk to report crimes and stolen or lost property.

If you need police help that is not urgent you can speak to an officer at the front desk of the station.

Under arrest

When a criminal or suspect has been arrested, he or she is taken to the police station. The suspect's fingerprints and photograph are taken. Then the person is put into a cell while they wait to be questioned about the crime.

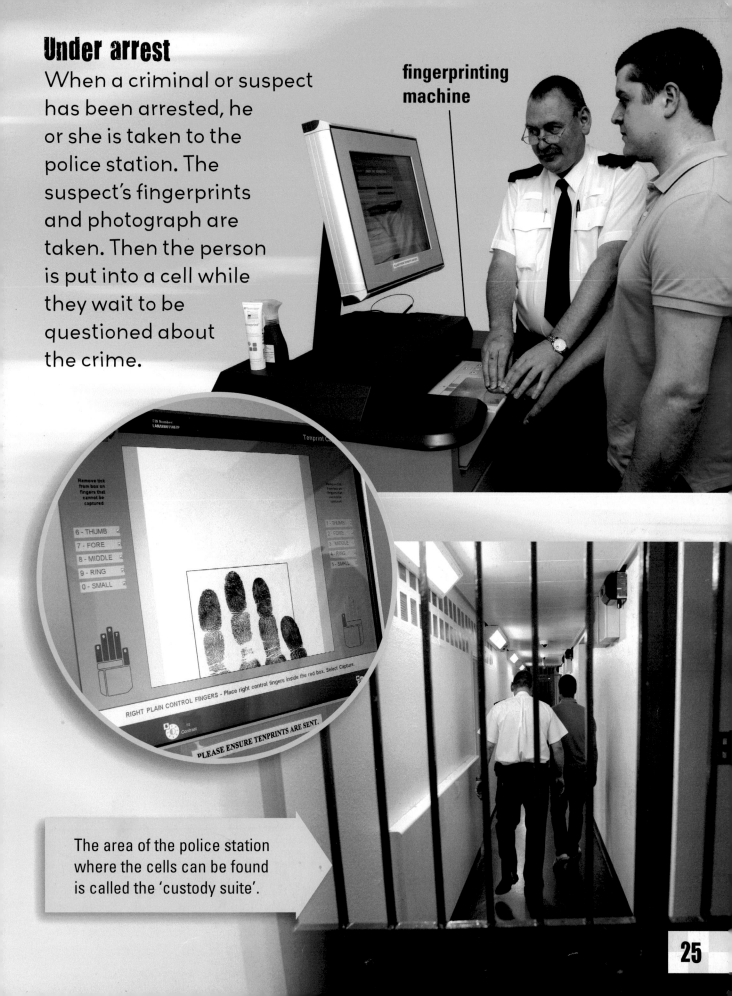

fingerprinting machine

Remove tick from box on fingers that cannot be captured

6 - THUMB
7 - FORE
8 - MIDDLE
9 - RING
0 - SMALL

1 - THUMB
2 - FORE
3 - MIDDLE
4 - RING
5 - SMALL

RIGHT PLAIN CONTROL FINGERS - Place right control fingers inside the red box. Select Capture.

PLEASE ENSURE TENPRINTS ARE SENT.

The area of the police station where the cells can be found is called the 'custody suite'.

KEEPING US SAFE

Police work is not all about dealing with accidents and crimes. It is also about preventing them happening. Officers spend time patrolling areas by car, bicycle or on foot. They look out for anything suspicious.

Patrolling can help prevent crime just by showing people that police are about.

Traffic police

Because many accidents happen on the roads, the police have a special section to deal with road safety and traffic accidents. Traffic police make sure that people obey the laws of the road and don't put lives in danger.

Police sometimes have to close a road or warn motorists of dangers on the road ahead.

Spreading the word

Part of police work is about teaching people how to stay safe. Officers visit schools to give talks about safety and explain when to make a 999 call.

FACE-TO-FACE

Sue – Police Constable

My shift starts at the police station where I change into my uniform and collect my equipment. Then I meet with the team to find out what I'm going to do. Some days I patrol an area on foot. While I'm out, I may get a radio call telling me to investigate an incident nearby. If it is serious, I can radio for help from other officers.

At the station, I sometimes spend time on the front desk or I may get called out to make an arrest. I never know what a shift will bring, so there's no chance of getting bored!

PROTECTING THE NEIGHBOURHOOD

Police Community Support Officers (PCSOs) do not have the same powers as other officers, but they are an important part of the police force. A PCSO's job is to make neighbourhoods safer and to stop anti-social behaviour – people behaving in ways that are harmful or upsetting to others.

A PCSO is a familiar face at the school gates and someone that children discuss problems with.

Keeping watch

PCSOs patrol the streets on foot or bicycle. Seeing them out on the streets makes people feel safer. PCSOs do not have the power to arrest people, but they can hand out fines for offences, such as cycling on a footpath, or dropping litter.

PCSOs may be radioed to go to a scene where anti-social behaviour has been reported or sent to people's houses to ask questions about an incident. PCSOs also give advice on how to prevent crime and work closely with **Neighbourhood Watch.** This is an organisation of local people who look out for crime in their neighbourhood.

999 Notes

Some buildings and lamp posts in the street are fitted with **closed-circuit television (CCTV)** cameras. These cameras record what happens in a particular place. They can help officers to spot criminals and record on film what they do.

CCTV camera

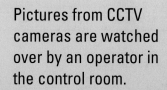

Pictures from CCTV cameras are watched over by an operator in the control room.

DO YOU HAVE WHAT IT TAKES?

To join the police force, you need to be at least 18 years old and have a driving licence. The first step is to fill in a police application form. Then you will take some written tests, fitness tests and have a medical examination to see if you are a suitable candidate.

If you are successful in all the tests, you might be offered a place in the police force. You will study and train and spend two years as a student officer. If that goes well, you may then go on to become a police officer.

Could you be a police officer?

Look at the following questions and answer 'yes' or 'no'.

- Do you work well as part of a team?
- Can you treat every person fairly and equally, no matter what they are like or what they have done?
- Are you willing to put yourself in situations that can be dangerous?
- Are you good at noticing details and remembering them?
- Are you willing to work night and day shifts, as well as weekends?
- Do you want to make life safer for other people?
- Can you stay calm in an emergency?
- Are you able to think and act quickly?
- Are you willing to take orders from more senior police officers?

If you have answered 'yes' to all these questions, then you may have what it takes to be a police officer.

GLOSSARY

anti-social behaviour acting in a way that is harmful, unpleasant or upsetting for others

arrest to stop someone and take them to a police station because police think they may have committed a crime

baton a stick carried by police officers that can be used as a weapon to protect themselves

closed-circuit television (CCTV) a system in which video is recorded by fixed cameras and sent to a set of television monitors

court a place where people decide whether or not someone has committed a crime

CS spray a spray used to stop someone getting away by making their eyes and nose hurt

dispatcher the person who sends police officers off to their destination in an emergency

DNA (deoxyribonucleic acid) a material present in all body cells that controls what a living thing looks like

evidence something that can be used to prove a fact

hoax a trick or joke to fool people into believing something is true

illegal not allowed by law

incident something that happens

laboratory a place with special equipment for carrying out scientific tests

landline a phone that is not a mobile

lifeline a line used by a diver for sending signals to the surface

Neighbourhood Watch a group of people living in an area who organise themselves to watch over each other's property and look out for crime

patrol to move about a particular area, watching and checking that everything is well

satellite navigation (sat nav) a piece of equipment used in vehicles to tell you how to get to a particular place

sergeant an officer who leads a team of police constables

shift the period of hours that a group of people work

suspect someone who police think may have broken the law

thermal imaging camera a camera that forms an image from heat given off by objects. For example, it can show an image of a person who is hiding or in the dark because the body gives off heat.

witness a person who has seen something happen

INDEX AND FURTHER INFORMATION

Websites

For a list of police websites in the UK, go to: **http://www.uk250.co.uk/Police/**

These web pages have lots of information written specially for young people
   by the Gloucestershire police:
   http://www.gloucestershire.police.uk/kids_aware/

Strathclyde Police have a great website for young people with lots of general
   information about the police force and fun activities. You'll find it at:
   http://www.spstation.com/

To find out more about the Neighbourhood Watch scheme, check out this website:
   http://www.neighbourhoodwatch.net/

Books

At the Police Station (Helping Hands), Ruth Thompson, Wayland, 2006
People Who Help Us: Police (Popcorn: People Who Help Us), Honor Head, Wayland 2010
The Police Station (Out and About), Sue Barraclough, Franklin Watts, 2006

EMERGENCY 999!

Contents of titles in series: